Saginaw Chippewa Academy LMC

JE   E PER
                                    42015

3 4050 0000 6046 2

D0847676

SAGINAW CHIPPEWA ACADEMY
LIBRARY MEDIA CENTER
MT. PLEASANT, MI 48858

SPLAT!

Written by
Mary Margaret Pérez-Mercado

Illustrated by
Richard L. Torrey

Children's Press ®
A Division of Grolier Publishing
New York • London • Hong Kong • Sydney
Danbury, Connecticut

With special love and thanks to my husband, daughters, friends,
and family who supported my love of writing.
—M.M.P.-M.

Reading Consultants
Linda Cornwell
Coordinator of School Quality and Professional Improvement
(Indiana State Teachers Association)

Katharine A. Kane
Education Consultant
(Retired, San Diego County Office of Education
and San Diego State University)

Visit Children's Press® on the Internet at:
http://publishing.grolier.com

Library of Congress Cataloguing-in-Publication Data
Pérez-Mercado, Mary Margaret.
    Splat! / written by Mary Margaret Pérez-Mercado ; illustrated by Richard L. Torre
        p. cm. – (Rookie reader)
    Summary: When a father and his daughter attempt to frost a cake together
more icing ends up around the room than on the cake.
    ISBN 0-516-21615-5 (lib.bdg.)   0-516-26543-1 (pbk.)
    [1. Icings, Cake Fiction. 2. Cake Fiction. 3. Fathers and daughters Fictic
4. Stories in rhyme.] I. Torrey, Rich, ill. II. Title. III. Series.
PZ8.3.M55167Sp 1999
{E]--dc21   99-22473
                                                   CIP

© 1999 by Children's Press®, a Division of Grolier Publishing Co.,In
Illustration © 1999 by Richard L. Torrey
All rights reserved. Published simultaneously in Canada.
Printed in the United States of America.
1 2 3 4 5 6 7 8 9 10 R 08 07 06 05 04 03 02 01 00 99

I helped my Dad.
We baked a cake.

I think it was
a big mistake.

4

The frosting fell.
It hit the floor.

It hit the wall.

It hit the door.

It hit the dog.

It hit the cat.

It hit my Dad
with one big . . .

SPL

19

It hit my Mom.

It hit my snake.

**But it NEVER EVER
hit the cake!**

23

WORD LIST (30 words)

a	fell	never
baked	floor	one
big	frosting	snake
but	helped	splat
cake	hit	the
cat	I	think
dad	it	wall
dog	mistake	was
door	mom	we
ever	my	with

About the Author

Mary Margaret Pérez-Mercado was born and raised in East Los Angeles. She received her B.A. from Cal-State L.A. and her M.L.S. from UCLA. She worked for the Los Angeles County Library System before becoming a youth services librarian for the Tucson-Pima Public Library. She lives with her husband and two daughters in Tucson, Arizona, where they enjoy watching the coyotes, javelinas, roadrunners, and jackrabbits that visit their backyard for drinks of water.

About the Illustrator

Richard L. Torrey has been an illustrator, syndicated cartoonist, and creator of a large line of greeting cards for the past fifteen years. He lives in Shoreham, New York, with his wife, Sue, and his children, Heather, 8, and Drew, 3.